Susan L. Lingo

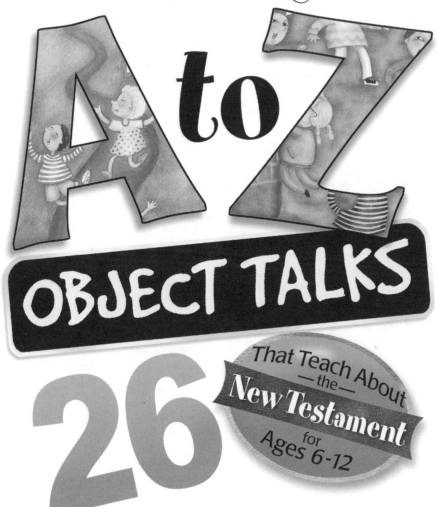

A to Z

OBJECT TALKS

26

That Teach About
—the—
New Testament
for
Ages 6-12

Memorable Messages
You~ ~~~~ Love!

D1114748

Standard
PUBLISHING
Bringing The Word to Life

Cincinnati, Ohio

DEDICATION

Get wisdom, get understanding;
do not forget my words or swerve from them.
Proverbs 4:5

A to Z Object Talks That Teach About the New Testament

Published by Standard Publishing, Cincinnati, Ohio
www.standardpub.com

Credits
Produced by Susan L. Lingo, Bright Ideas Books™
Illustrated by Jason Lynch
Cover design by Liz Howe

10 09 08   8

ISBN-13: 978-0-7847-1237-5
ISBN-10: 0-7847-1237-9

CONTENTS

INTRODUCTION

What's so amazing about a tiny mustard seed?
How much was a "lepton" worth?
Who wore "kaffiyehs,"
and how did they keep them on their heads?

The answers from A to Z are found in *A to Z Object Talks That Teach About the New Testament!* Kids will love making edible dough hearts as they learn how God molds their lives. They'll delight their friends wearing outstanding outer garments that remind them of giving to others. And kids will understand how the sweetness of our prayers rises to God as they make sweet-smelling incense. *A to Z Object Talks That Teach About the New Testament* combines life-changing Bible truths with tons of neat New Testament trivia to bring the New Testament awesomely alive and to make it radically relevant for kids today.

Each memorable message in *A to Z Object Talks That Teach About the New Testament* introduces an important biblical theme, such as Jesus' grace, forgiveness, growing strong faith, and praising Christ. Kids interact with each message by reading from the Bible, discussing the importance of each theme, and making cool crafts or super snacks as reminders of the New Testament and its powerful Bible truths. Kids come away from these meaningful messages filled with

- **powerful reminders of God's Word,**
- **appreciation for the New Testament,**
- **fascinating facts and too-cool Bible trivia, and**
- **a sense of community and teamwork.**

Use these motivating object talks as mini lessons on New Testament truths, as cool stand-alone object talks or kids' sermons, or as powerful Bible-story enrichment tools. Make every moment with your kids count as you present memorable messages, fascinating facts, and awesome Bible enrichment from A to Z!

A ANGEL

We can be messengers for Jesus.
Matthew 28:5, 6, 19, 20; Luke 2:9, 10

A TO Z SUPPLIES: You'll need a Bible, an angel figurine, a wallpaper sample book (available free from home-center stores), fine-tipped permanent markers, thick chenille wires, 1-inch wooden beads (available at craft stores), and glitter glue.

Before class, collect old wallpaper sample books. You'll need the kinds that have full-size pages (at least 10-by-12-inches). If you have extra wallpaper rolls, cut a 10-by-12-inch rectangle for each child.

SPELLING IT OUT

Place the angel figurine behind you and tell kids you have a riddle for them to guess. Repeat the following riddle, then ask kids who they think you're describing:

> *I have a very important role—*
> *When you know, just give a nod—*
> *I've been charged with watching over God's people*
> *And being a messenger for God!*
> *Who am I?*

When kids guess that you're describing an angel, say: **We read about angels many times in the Bible. Perhaps the most well-known time was during Jesus' birth.** *Angel* **begins with the letter A, and today we'll discover who angels are and what their important jobs are. We'll also learn that we can be special messengers for Jesus.**

Hold up the angel figurine and say: **God's angels brought heavenly news to many people in the Bible. When Mary was to become the mother of Jesus, an angel told her the good news. It was three angels who told Abraham that Sarah would give birth to Isaac. And it was an angel who led Peter out of prison chains. God has sent angels to protect his people. And God sent angels to carry his important news. Let's discover what the most important news that angels ever brought to earth might have been.**

READING THE WORD

Invite volunteers to read aloud Luke 2:9, 10 and Matthew 28:5, 6, 19, and 20. Then ask:

- **Why was it so important to tell news about Jesus and his birth? Jesus' resurrection?**
- **Why is it important for us to bring news about Jesus to others?**
- **What important things could you tell about Jesus?**

Say: **God sent angels to earth to protect his people and to act as his heavenly messengers. We can carry important news about Jesus to others, too. When we tell others about Jesus' forgiveness, love, and salvation, we're like heavenly messengers on a mission! We can make awesome angels to remind us of the importance of being messengers carrying the Good News about Jesus.**

Show kids how to accordion fold a sheet of wallpaper. Turn the folded paper lengthwise and loosely wrap one half of a thick chenille wire around the center of the paper to make a body and wings (the body is the wire, the wings are the folded wallpaper). Next, thread a wooden bead through the other end of the chenille wire and wrap the wire around the base of the bead to hold the angel's "head" in place. Use markers to add facial features and glitter glue to make a halo.

End with a prayer asking God to help make you his messengers in telling others about Jesus.

BAPTISM

We can believe and accept Jesus.
Matthew 28:19; Mark 16:16; Acts 16:31

A TO Z SUPPLIES: You'll need a Bible, sponges, fine-tipped permanent markers, and a bowl of water.

Before class, cut sponges into 3-inch squares, one for each child plus one extra. Arrange to have a children's minister or church leader to visit with your children about how baptism is performed and viewed in relation to your church.

SPELLING IT OUT

Set out the bowl of water and hold up a square of sponge. Ask kids to name different ways the sponge can be soaked with water. Suggestions might include dipping it in water or sprinkling it thoroughly. Say: **If we want a sponge to be completely covered with water, the best way is probably dunking or immersing the sponge in water. Just as sponges are covered and immersed in water to be filled, Christians want to be covered and filled with Jesus. One of our symbolic ways to be covered and new in Christ is called baptism.** *Baptism* **begins with the letter B, and today we'll discover what baptism means and why Jesus wants us to be baptized as Christians who want to be covered and made new in Christ.**

John the Baptist was the first person the Bible tells about who baptized people and made them clean and ready for accepting Jesus. John called the people to ask for forgiveness of their sins and to be washed clean. Jesus came to John the Baptist to be baptized. Jesus had no sin to ask forgiveness for, but God wanted Jesus to make himself ready for his ministry and to provide a powerful example of baptism for us. In fact, when Jesus was baptized, God said, "This is my Son, whom I love; with him I am well pleased" (Matthew 3:17). Ask:

- Why do you think Jesus' baptism pleased God?
- Why did Jesus want to obey his Father in heaven?

READING THE WORD

Read aloud Matthew 28:19; Mark 16:16; and Acts 16:31. This may be a good time to introduce your children's minister or church leader to talk about baptism. Continue: **Jesus commanded us to go into the world and bring people into the kingdom of heaven through baptizing them in the name of the Father, Son, and Holy Spirit. In other words, Jesus wants us all to be baptized so we can receive his forgiveness and be saved from sin and eternal death. What a gift we receive through baptism!** Ask:

- How can being baptized show our love for Jesus? our obedience to God?
- In what ways are we changed and made clean after accepting Jesus into our lives and being baptized?

Say: **When we're baptized and ask forgiveness of our sins and repent, we're telling the Lord and others that we want to live with Jesus as the Lord of our lives! Let's make these sponges as reminders that when we believe in Jesus and are baptized we become clean in Christ.**

Have kids use permanent markers to write "Be clean in Christ" on their sponge squares. Then end with a prayer thanking the Lord for baptism and for the chance to believe and be saved.

COINS
We want to appreciate God's gifts.
Matthew 5:42; 10:8; Luke 16:10-12

A TO Z SUPPLIES: You'll need a Bible, a variety of coins (pennies, quarters, dimes, and nickels), photocopies of the coins from the margin, paper plates and bowls, plastic forks, salad dressing, and a variety of sliced vegetable "coins," including round cucumber slices, carrots slices, and cherry tomato slices.

Before class, photocopy the coins in the margin on stiff paper and cut them out. Cut uncooked vegetables into round slices to look like tasty coins. If your kids are older, let them do the slicing with plastic knives. Place the vegetable coins in three bowls.

SPELLING IT OUT

Hold up the coins and challenge kids to identify the coins and tell what each is worth. (For extra fun, also bring in foreign coins that kids might not recognize.) Then invite kids to tell what things we can do or buy with money. Say: **Coins are important because they represent money. Money is what we use to buy food, clothing, and other items we need to survive.** *Coins* **begins with the letter C, and today we'll discover that coins were very important in New Testament times as well. We'll also learn what it means to be good stewards with the gifts of money God gives us.**

Coins are mentioned quite often in the Bible. For example, once Jesus told Peter to open a fish's mouth, and there was a coin inside. In another Bible story, we read about a poor widow giving the only coins she had to serve God. Coins in New Testament times were much different from what they are today. Here are what some coins of biblical days looked like.

Pass the paper coins and continue: **Coins were made from bronze, silver, copper, or gold, and there were so many different types of coins that it was important for buyers and sellers to agree on how much each coin was worth. The coin you're looking at, called a lepton, was made of bronze or copper and was worth only a few cents. Most people didn't have a lot of money, so when someone had coins, they were precious and used for important things such as taxes, food, and helping the poor. The people knew it was good to appreciate the gifts and money God provided!** Ask:
- How can money help other people? serve God?
- Why do you think it's good to appreciate what God gives us?

Say: **Let's see what the Bible says about taking care of what God gives us and also about helping others with our gifts and treasures.**

READING THE WORD

Read aloud Matthew 10:8b and Luke 16:10-12. Then say: **When we take good care of money and use it in wise ways, we're being good stewards of our money. God wants us to be good stewards of our money and not waste it or spend it foolishly.** Ask:
- Why do you think God wants us to be good stewards?
- How can being a good steward allow us to help others? to serve God?
- What could you do with money to help poor or hungry people?

Say: **If you have a treasure, you don't toss it away—you take good care of it. That's just how it should be with our money. When God blesses us with money, we don't want to toss it away on wasteful things we don't need when so many people need our help. We can be good stewards and use our gifts and money to help others and serve God at the same time. And that feels good! Now let's make**

N
O
P
Q
R
S
T
U
V
W
X
Y
Z

crunchy coin salads that taste good and will help us remember to be good stewards of our money.

Set out the bowls of vegetable coins and let kids place a few of each on paper plates. Add a bit of salad dressing for extra flavor. Before eating, share a prayer thanking God for all his gifts and asking for his help in making you good stewards. As kids leave, encourage them to think of ways they will be good stewards whenever they enjoy similar vegetables at home.

DATES
We can be God's good fruit.
Luke 6:45; Galatians 5:22, 23

A TO Z SUPPLIES: You'll need a Bible; dried, pitted dates; plastic knives; napkins; and softened cream cheese.

Before class, you may wish to locate a picture of a palm tree or a date palm. You'll need two dried, pitted dates for each child.

SPELLING IT OUT

Ask kids to name their favorite fruits. Then hold up a dried, pitted date and see if kids can identify this kind of fruit. Say: **This is a dried date. Dried dates are sweet and chewy and were enjoyed often in New Testament times. *Date* begins with the letter D, and today we'll discover more about dates and the palm trees on which they grow. We'll also learn about what it means to be God's good fruit.**

Dates grow on a huge type of palm tree. When the date palm grows for several years, it sends out long shoots, and on the ends of these shoots grow clusters of dates. Dates were eaten raw, or sometimes they were cooked with other fruits to make a paste to enjoy with bread. Dates were often laid on a clean cloth on the ground and allowed to dry for several days in the hot sun. Women placed thin cloths over the dates to keep insects away and turned the dates often as they dried. Dried dates were a great treat to take on long trips because they lasted for months without spoiling. What's most amazing is that a good palm tree could produce nutritious dates for over two hundred years! That's a lot of good fruit, isn't it? Ask:

■ **What does fruit do for us?**

■ **How does good fruit produce more good fruit?**

Say: **Good fruit feeds us and gives us energy to do things. And good fruit also produces more good fruit to feed lots of people. Let's see what the Bible says about good fruit and about being God's good fruit.**

READING THE WORD

Invite volunteers to read aloud Luke 6:45; Matthew 3:10; and Galatians 5:22, 23. Then ask:

■ **In what ways are we like God's good fruit?**

■ **Why is it important to serve others and God?**

■ **How can we produce good fruit in our lives?**

■ **In what ways can we share good fruit with others**?

Have kids tell that obeying God, reading the Bible, being kind to others, and teaching others about Jesus are all ways to grow and share good fruit. Then say: **God wants us to grow good fruit in our lives. As Galatians 5:22, 23 teaches us, good fruit includes love, joy, peace, patience, kindness, goodness, faithfulness, gentleness, and self-control. When we grow these good things in our lives, we can put them to use helping others and serving God.**

To help us remember that we can be God's good fruit, let's make Good Fruit Dates. You can make two date treats: one to keep and one to share! Show kids how to gently part the pitted dates and use their plastic knives to stuff the dates with softened cream cheese. Place the dates on napkins. Have kids find partners to exchange dates with. Then offer a prayer to God asking for his help in finding ways to grow good fruit in their lives to share with others.

EPISTLES
We can tell others about Jesus.
Matthew 28:19; 1 Thessalonians 2:8

A TO Z SUPPLIES: You'll need a Bible, a letter in a sealed envelope, stationery, envelopes, newsprint, and pens or pencils.

Before class, write the following on a sheet of paper and place it in a sealed envelope addressed to the class. "Dear kids,

the best friend we could ever have in the whole world is Jesus. Spread the good news! Love, (Your Name)." Be sure you have an envelope for each child. Also, you'll need to write the titles of the New Testament letters (Romans through Jude). Place the list where kids can see it.

SPELLING IT OUT

Gather kids and hold up the letter in the sealed envelope. Say: **I have a letter, and it's a very important letter for you all. We'll open it later, but first tell me, why do people send letters?** Allow time for kids to respond, then continue: **Did you know that almost a third of the New Testament is made up of letters? The letters in the Bible are called "epistles," which begins with the letter E. Today we'll learn what the New Testament epistles tell us and how we can tell others some important news of our own.**

There are twenty-one epistles in the New Testament. Let's read the names of these epistles together. Read the names of the New Testament letters from the newsprint. Then say: **Do you recognize some of these names? These are all the letters, or epistles, found in the New Testament. The epistles are letters written by different people to teach others about God, Jesus, people, and the church. Some of the epistles were written by the apostle Paul; others were written by Peter and John. The letters teach us about remembering how God is love and about obeying him. They talk about the power of Jesus' death and resurrection and how we can have eternal life when we accept Jesus. And the New Testament letters tell us how to be helpful, loving Christians who serve one another and bring others to Jesus. Let's read a few verses from several of the epistles.**

READING THE WORD

Invite volunteers to read aloud 1 Thessalonians 2:8 and Jude 3. Then say: **Wow! Those are awesome verses—they tell why others wanted to spread the news about Jesus. The epistles encourage us and help us learn more about Jesus and about following him. Letters are for telling important news, and that's exactly what the epistles do for us.** Ask:

- **Why did the writers of the epistles think their news was important?**

- How can reading the epistles help us be more like Jesus wants us to be?
- What could you tell someone in a letter about Jesus?

Say: **The New Testament epistles begin with greetings to fellow Christians and praises to the Lord.** (Choose an epistle and read several verses from the greeting.) **Then the letters went on to teach us about Jesus and our relationship with him. And finally, the letters ended with closings that praise Jesus.** (Read a closing from one of the epistles.)

We can learn so much about Jesus from the New Testament epistles, and we can write our own epistles to tell others about Jesus, just as he told us. Read Matthew 18:19, then hand out sheets of stationery and pens or pencils. Invite kids to write a one-sentence greeting that offers praise to Jesus and then three sentences that tell about Jesus. Finally, have kids write one sentence that praises Jesus once again. Tell children to sign their letters and place them in envelopes. Challenge kids to hand the letter to someone during the week to read. End by reading the letter you had sealed in your envelope.

FISHING
We can be fishers of men.
Matthew 4:19; Mark 16:15

A TO Z SUPPLIES: You'll need a Bible, a fishing pole (with no hook), a small rubber ball, plastic sandwich bags, twist-tie wires, markers, colored tissue paper, craft glue, googly eyes (from craft stores), and five slips of paper for each child.

Before class, write the words to Matthew 4:19 on a slip of paper. Tape the slip of paper to the end of the fishing line with a small rubber ball for weight.

SPELLING IT OUT

Gather kids in the center of the room and tell them that you're going fishing. Explain that they'll be the "fish" and you'll try to catch one of them. Stand at one end of the room and gently cast your line into the midst of the fish. Have the child nearest the fishing line hold on as you "reel" him in. After the child reads the verse silently, cast the line for the next catch.

N O P Q R S T U V W X Y Z

When everyone has been "caught" and has read the verse, say: **Fishing is fun—especially when we fish for Jesus! What do you think Matthew 4:19 means when it says to be "fishers of men"?** Allow time for responses, then say: **When we follow Jesus as our fishing guide and fish for people, we tell them about Jesus and his forgiving love. We want to bring others to Jesus.** *Fishing* **begins with the letter F, and today we'll explore fishing in New Testament times as we learn about what it meant to fish for men.**

Since most people in Jesus' day couldn't afford fresh meat, they fished or purchased fish for their meals. Men would toss nets into the sea to pull in their catch. We know that Jesus roasted fish to eat, as John 21:9 tells us. (Read the verse aloud.) **Fish were often salted and smoked so they wouldn't spoil in the heat. Jesus knew how important fishing was to the people, and he used fishing to describe how his disciples could win people for the Lord.**

READING THE WORD

Read aloud Matthew 4:19, then say: **Jesus wanted others to know the truths he was teaching about God, his love, and his forgiveness. Jesus wanted people to learn about God and to follow him. And Jesus used fishing as a way to describe to his disciples how he wanted to bring people to him.** Ask:

■ **How is fishing for people like fishing for fish?**
■ **How does telling others about Jesus help them?**
■ **What can you do to lead others to Jesus?**

Read Mark 16:15 and Acts 1:8. Say: **Jesus wanted us to be fishermen—but not for fish. Jesus wanted us to tell others the truths he taught so other people would know and follow Jesus. We can be fishers of men by telling others about Jesus' love and forgiveness. Let's make fancy fish to fish for people and tell them about Jesus.**

Hand each child five slips of paper. Have kids write sentences telling about Jesus on their slips. Sentences might include "Jesus loves us," "Jesus forgives us when we ask him," and "Jesus teaches us God's truth." Stuff colored tissue paper loosely into the plastic bags, then slide the slips of paper inside the "fish." Seal the top of the bags using twist-tie wires. Glue googly eyes on the fish, and add tissue-paper fins.

Tell kids to give their fish to someone and have them read a slip of paper before passing the fish to someone else. Challenge kids to "fish" for neighbors, friends, and family members by telling them all about Jesus.

GETHSEMANE
We can pray as Jesus prayed.
Luke 22:44; John 17:11, 20, 21

A TO Z SUPPLIES: You'll need a Bible, green olives, self-sealing plastic sandwich bags, red construction paper, scissors, and cotton swabs.

Before class, be sure you have three or four green olives for each child—one to eat and the others to squeeze for oil.

SPELLING IT OUT

Distribute the self-sealing sandwich bags and have each child place three or four olives in the bag. As kids work, invite them to tell what the green objects are and what they're used for or in. Then say: **Olives grow around the world, but they grow in abundance in biblical lands. There were many olive groves and gardens in New Testament times; one of the most well known is the Garden of Gethsemane, which is where Jesus offered his very last prayer for us. *Gethsemane* begins with the letter G, and today we'll learn about Gethsemane and why it was an appropriate place for Jesus to offer this powerful prayer of love. We'll also discover that we can pray for others just as Jesus did.**

Invite kids to eat one olive and say: **As early as the Old Testament times, God's people used olive oil for special worship and prayers. Olive oil was daubed on foreheads as a special anointing, as when Samuel anointed David as the next king of Israel. Olive oil came from being pressed in oil presses. The word *Gethsemane* means "oil press," and there was probably an oil press near the garden. Olives were dumped into a large stone vat and a plank of wood placed over the olives. A heavy stone or small boulder was placed on the plank, and its pressure squeezed**

the oil from the olives. **See if you can apply pressure on the olives in your bag and squeeze a bit of oil from them.**

Have kids seal their plastic bags, then press on the olives with the palms of their hands on a hard, flat surface. When the oil is squeezed from the olives, let kids feel its texture. Then continue: **Jesus chose to pray for us in the olive garden called Gethsemane, and it was here that he prayed about the great pressure of the world's sins he would bear on the cross. In fact, the pressure was so great that Jesus' sweat fell like drops of blood!** Ask:

- **Why did Jesus feel enormous pressure in the garden?**
- **What do you imagine Jesus prayed for us?**

Let's read a bit of Jesus' powerful, loving prayer for us.

READING THE WORD

Invite volunteers to read aloud Luke 22:42 and John 17:11, 20, 21. Then say: **Jesus knew God's plan was for him to die on the cross so we could be forgiven. Jesus knew he had to bear the weight of the world's sins so we could live as God's friends.**

- **In what ways was Jesus' prayer unselfish? courageous? full of love?**
- **What can we learn about praying for others through Jesus' example?**

Say: **Even when Jesus was facing the scariest, most difficult time in his life, he stopped to pray for us in the quiet Garden of Gethsemane. That is amazing, isn't it? And we can pray for others, too.** Ask:

- **In what ways can our prayers help others?**
- **How do our prayers for others demonstrate our love?**

Let's make prayer hearts to remind us of the love Jesus felt when he prayed for us in Gethsemane—and for the love we show when we pray for others.

Have kids cut 6-inch construction-paper hearts. Show kids how to dip cotton swabs in the olive oil in their plastic bags and write "Jesus prayed for us" on their hearts. Explain that the oil will remind them how Jesus prayed for us even though he was pressed down by the weight of the world's sins. Encourage kids to hold their paper hearts each day and choose one person to pray for. End with a prayer thanking Jesus for caring enough to pray for us on that very hard night in the Garden of Gethsemane.

HEALING

Jesus heals us.
Psalm 147:3; Matthew 13:15; Acts 9:34

A TO Z SUPPLIES: You'll need a Bible, plastic bandages, tape, red construction paper, and markers.

Before class, be sure you have one plastic bandage for each child. Cut out a 6-inch red paper heart for each child.

SPELLING IT OUT

Hold up a plastic bandage and invite kids to tell about times they've been sick or hurt. Encourage them to tell how it felt to have someone help them during these times. After several kids share, say: **When we speak of someone needing healing, we usually think of their physical bodies. We tend to think of skinned knees or broken arms or catching a cold as times when we need to be healed. But did you know that hearts sometimes need healing, too?** Hand each child a paper heart. Continue: **Sometimes our feelings are hurt by words or disappointments. Think of a time your heart needed healing, then tear your paper heart in half.**

Allow time for kids to tear the paper hearts, then say: *Healing* **begins with the letter H, and today we'll learn about healing in the New Testament and how Jesus heals us today. In New Testament times, there were more diseases than doctors. Many doctors used awful magic spells or even poison to treat their patients. A cure for corns on someone's feet was to place coins under the toes. Did it work? Probably not! But many people had faith that Jesus could help them and heal them through God's power, so they sought him out. Just as Jesus loves us all in different ways, he healed people in different ways, too. For example, once Jesus healed a blind man by spitting on the ground and putting mud on the man's eyes. Another time, he healed ten lepers—but only one man thought to thank him.**

READING THE WORD

Ask a volunteer to read aloud Psalm 147:3; Matthew 13:15; and Acts 9:34. Then say: **Jesus healed bodies, and he**

N
O
P
Q
R
S
T
U
V
W
X
Y
Z

healed broken hearts and spirits, too. And Jesus continues to heal us today. When we trust Jesus and look to him for healing, we become healed in many different ways. Ask:

- What does a mended heart and spirit feel like?
- How can loving and trusting Jesus help us feel better?
- In what ways can we be healed through loving Jesus?

Say: **Sometimes we're not healed in exactly the way that we might like or believe we should be, but that's where trusting the Lord comes in. He knows best how to heal us, and our faith in Jesus allows his healing power to work. Let's offer a prayer thanking Jesus for his healing love. We'll use our torn paper hearts and these bandages to help.**

Pray: **Dear Lord, we're so glad your power and love can heal us in so many ways. Right now I ask healing for** (have kids silently think of a healing need, then "tape" the paper hearts together with plastic bandages). **By your power and love we are healed. Thank you, Lord. Amen.**

INCENSE
Our prayers rise to God and please him.
Luke 1:10; Revelation 5:8

A TO Z SUPPLIES: You'll need a Bible, incense sticks, matches, a ceramic dish or saucer, small index cards and pens, self-sealing sandwich bags, cloves, powdered cinnamon or cinnamon sticks, orange rinds, and ribbon.

Before class, cut the index cards and several incense sticks in half and cut a 10-inch length of ribbon for each child.

SPELLING IT OUT

Gather kids and ask them to name scents and smells that are pleasing to them. Suggestions might include hot chocolate, a loved one's perfume or cologne, freshly laundered clothing, or roses. After everyone has had a chance to call out a scent, say: **There are many scents that are pleasing to us. Here's one you may like also!** Light the incense stick and wave it gently around the room. When it starts to form an ash, hold the stick over the saucer or ceramic dish.

Say: **This is called incense, which begins with the letter I and is the subject of our talk for today. Incense was used a great deal in both the Old and New Testaments. In the Old Testament, incense was used for worshiping God and to scent the tabernacles and tents where God was honored and praised. In the New Testament, incense was also used as a way to honor God and was often given as a special and expensive gift. Who brought incense to Jesus when he was born?** Pause for kids to tell that it was the Magi who brought Jesus the gift of frankincense.

Say: **See how the incense rises upward? Let's read a few New Testament verses that compare rising incense to something we all do. When you think you know what that is, fold your hands and hold them high.**

READING THE WORD

Read aloud Luke 1:10 and Revelation 5:8b. Then ask:

- **What rises to God as incense rises in the air?**
- **How do you think God feels when our prayers rise to him?**
- **In what ways are our prayers pleasing to God the way rising incense is pleasing to smell?**

Say: **Our prayers are so important to God! And our prayers to God are pleasing to him. When we pray, our feelings, thoughts, words, and desires rise to God's ears as incense rises in the air—and God hears! God hears our prayers, and they please him!** Ask:

- **How is God hearing our prayers a demonstration of his love?**
- **In what ways does prayer show that we love God?**
- **What prayers could you let rise to God today?**

Say: **When we take the time to pray to God, our prayers rise to him in a cloud of love! And God hears every prayer and is pleased by them. Let's make some pretty prayer potpourri to remind us that our prayers are like a sweet scent rising to God!**

Set the craft items, pieces of incense, and spices on a table. Hand each child an index card and pen. Challenge kids to write brief prayer requests on the cards. Then have kids prepare potpourri bags by placing several cloves, one or two pieces of incense, a few orange peels, and a cinnamon stick or sprinkling of cinnamon in each bag. Tell kids to place their

prayer-request cards in the bags, then form a circle. Lead kids in a prayer thanking God for hearing prayers, then open your prayer potpourri bags to let the scent of the spices rise with your prayers to God.

Close by handing kids ribbons to tie around their bags. Tell them to pray tonight and then open their prayer potpourri bags and smell the sweetness as it rises to God with their prayers!

JESUS

We call on the name of Jesus for help.
Matthew 1:23; Philippians 2:9-11

A TO Z SUPPLIES: You'll need Bibles, markers, white poster board, tape, and newsprint.

Before class, cut a 10-inch poster-board square for each child. Tape the newsprint to the wall or a door and place a marker nearby.

SPELLING IT OUT

Gather kids by the newsprint and say: **We all know that Jesus is God's only Son who came to love and forgive us so we could live forever in heaven. But Jesus was known by many different names that told more about who Jesus is and what he can do. The name *Jesus* begins with the letter J, and today we'll discover how to call on the name of Jesus as well as what other names Jesus is known by in the Bible. We'll also learn that calling on the name of Jesus brings special help and comfort.**

The name Jesus means "God saves." Jesus was also called Immanuel, which means "God with us." Read aloud Matthew 1:23, then say: **I'll write Jesus' name on this paper, and as we find other names for the Lord, we'll list them here. Get with a partner and let's look in the Bible to find more names for Jesus.** When kids are in pairs, have them look up and read the following verses, then list the names or expressions for Jesus on the newsprint. Take a moment to briefly discuss what each name tells about Jesus or his power.

- ■ *John 6:35* ("bread of life")
- ■ *Revelation 19:16* ("King of kings and Lord of lords")

- **_Luke 2:11_** ("Savior")
- **_Matthew 14:33_** ("Son of God")
- **_Luke 19:10_** ("Son of Man")
- **_John 10:11_** ("good shepherd")
- **_John 14:6_** ("the way and the truth and the life")
- **_Isaiah 9:6_** ("Prince of Peace")
- **_Luke 1:32_** ("Son of the Most High")

When the names are listed on the newsprint, say: **Wow! What a great list of names for Jesus! The Bible has even more, and if you're good detectives you can find them. These names tell us about who Jesus is and what Jesus does. Remember how the name _Jesus_ means "God saves"? Let's see how calling on the wonderful name of Jesus helps and saves us.**

READING THE WORD

Ask volunteers to read aloud John 20:31 and Philippians 2:9-11. Then say: **Calling on Jesus' name lets him know that we trust him and know he is with us.** Ask:

- **How can calling on the name of Jesus help us in times of trouble?**
- **How can calling on the name of Jesus help us praise and honor him?**

Say: **Jesus' name is awesome and has awesome power! In fact, Philippians 2:9-11 tells us that at the name of Jesus, every knee will bow and tongue confess that he is Lord! That's pretty powerful, isn't it? Let's make power posters of the names of Jesus to remind us of the many ways we can call on Jesus' name.**

Have children use markers and the poster-board squares to make graphic designs of the names for Christ from your list on the wall. Challenge kids to be creative in how they form the letters. If you want, have kids write the Scripture reference for each name either beside or under it.

End with a prayer thanking Jesus for giving us help and saving us through his powerful name.

KAFFIYEH

**The Lord covers and protects us.
Psalm 91:1-6; Ephesians 6:10, 11**

A TO Z SUPPLIES: You'll need a Bible, several hats or
scarves, permanent markers, rope or woven cord, scissors, and
white cotton fabric.

*Before class, cut a 3-foot square of inexpensive white cotton
cloth for each child. You'll also need to cut a 2-foot length of
rope or cord for each child.*

SPELLING IT OUT

Sit in a circle and have kids place the hats or scarves on
their heads and tell one reason people wear head coverings.
Then pass the hats around the circle until you say "stop." Have
the kids holding the hats place them on their heads and give
another reason people wear hats or scarves. Continue until
everyone has worn a hat and given a reason for headgear.

Say: **Headgear is worn for a number of different rea-
sons, and even back in New Testament times people wore
things to cover their heads. One of the items they wore
was called a "kaffiyeh."** *Kaffiyeh* **begins with the letter K,
and today we'll see how a kaffiyeh was made and why it
was worn. We'll also discover how Jesus' love is like a kaffiyeh that covers and protects us.**

Hold up a square of cotton fabric. Say: **Headgear in Jesus'
day was made of simple materials such as this square of
cotton. A kaffiyeh, or head-square, was made by folding a
large square of cotton into a triangle.** Fold the fabric into a
triangle and place it on your head with the point stretching
down the back of your neck. **The kaffiyeh was held in place
by wrapping a rope or cord gently around the head.** Wrap
a length of rope around your head and forehead and loosely
tie it in place. **The kaffiyeh covered and protected the
wearer's head from wind, dust, insects, and sun. We don't
see many paintings of Jesus wearing head coverings, but
it's almost certain that he did.** Ask:

■ **How did kaffiyehs protect people who wore them?**
■ **What happened if people forgot to wear their kaffiyehs or other headgear?**

■ In what ways is this like forgetting to keep God's Word or Jesus' love near us every day?

READING THE WORD

Read aloud Psalm 91:1-6 and Ephesians 6:10, 11. Say: **Isn't is wonderful that the Lord covers and protects us with his love and truth? But we must remember to keep God's Word and Jesus' love close in our hearts just as people in Jesus' day had to remember to put on their kaffiyehs for protection. When we know God's Word and follow Jesus, we're power protected!** Ask:

■ **In what ways does God's Word protect us?**

■ **How does Christ's love cover us?**

■ **What would happen without the Lord protecting and covering us?**

■ **How does knowing you're covered and protected help you every day?**

Say: **Without the Lord's covering and protection, we'd be in real trouble. But when we allow the Lord to be first in our lives and obey him, he covers and protects us with love, truth, and strength. Let's make kaffiyehs as a reminder of how the Lord covers us.**

Invite kids to use permanent markers to decorate the squares of cotton fabric. Have kids write "God covers us" on their kaffiyehs. Then help kids place the kaffiyehs on their heads and to gently tie them using lengths of rope or cord. End with a prayer thanking the Lord for covering and protecting us with his love, power, strength, and truth.

 # LEPER
Jesus heals us in many ways.
Exodus 15:26; Matthew 4:23; 8:2, 3

A TO Z SUPPLIES: You'll need a Bible, red self-adhesive dots (available at office supply stores), index cards, markers, construction paper, and glue.

Before class, be sure you have several packages of red self-adhesive dots. Each person will need three of the sticky dots.

N O P Q R S T U V W X Y Z

SPELLING IT OUT

Hand each child three red sticky dots and explain that you are going play a quick game of Spots-n-Dots. When you say "go," kids are to try and tag three other people with the dots by sticking them to their arms, shoes, or hands (not faces). If someone is tagged and wants to remove a dot, she can try to stick that dot to someone else. Tell kids that they have one minute to play Spots-n-Dots.

After a minute, call time and have everyone count the spots-n-dots that are stuck to them. Then ask children to name illnesses or conditions that involve red spots. Suggestions are sure to include measles, chicken pox, chigger and mosquito bites, and even hives.

Say: **Having red spots on our skin isn't very pleasant, is it? Chicken pox and measles can spread to other people, so we usually stay away from infected people until they're feeling better and are less "dotty." In Bible times, there was another skin disease, called leprosy, and it was easy to catch. People who had leprosy were called lepers. *Lepers* begins with the letter L, and today we'll discover a bit about leprosy and why it was such a miracle when Jesus cured lepers. We'll also discover that Jesus heals us in many ways. We'll use our red dots later, so leave them where they're stuck for now.**

Leprosy was caused by bacteria that made the skin turn red, spotty, and oozy. In bad cases, leprosy even affected people's nerves and how their legs moved. People were afraid of lepers because they didn't want to catch this terrible disease. So lepers were sent to live by themselves. Ask:

■ **How do you suppose it felt to be a leper and be sent away?**

■ **How were the lepers affected on the outsides of their bodies? How were their feelings inside affected?**

Say: **The worst part about leprosy was that there was no cure. Nothing could take away the suffering of the lepers. Nothing until Jesus, that is!**

READING THE WORD

Invite several volunteers to read aloud Exodus 15:26 and Matthew 4:23; 8:2, 3. Then ask:

■ **Why did Jesus want to help and heal the lepers?**

- How did Jesus heal the lepers on the outside? on the inside?
- In what ways did Jesus' miracle of healing show his love for the lepers?

Say: **Jesus loves us and wants us to be healthy and happy, and Jesus can heal us through God's power. Jesus healed the skin of the lepers and, in doing so, he also healed their sad hearts! Jesus helps and heals us in many ways!**

Let's make neat get-well cards to help someone else who may be feeling ill or sad. We'll use your red dots on the cards and turn them into cool pictures such as red balloons, flowers, or polka-dot designs. Show kids how to fold a half sheet of construction paper and glue an index card inside. Use markers to decorate the outsides of the cards, then write cheery messages such as "Jesus heals our hurts and hearts" inside on the index cards. After the cards are complete, challenge kids to hand them to someone who could use a reminder of Jesus' love and their own caring.

MUSTARD SEED
Faith is a growing thing!
Matthew 17:20; Luke 17:5, 6

A TO Z SUPPLIES: You'll need a Bible, mustard seeds, cotton balls, clear plastic vials, satin cord, tape, water, and fine-tipped permanent markers.

Before class, be sure you have a mustard seed or two for each child plus a couple of extras. Mustard seeds can be purchased in spice departments or gardening centers. Cut satin cord into 18-inch lengths.

SPELLING IT OUT

Hold several mustard seeds in your hand and ask kids to identify what helps seeds grow into large plants and trees. Say: **When we think of seeds, we often think of growing things. From tiny seeds grow beautiful flowers, lush plants, and leafy trees. These seeds are mustard seeds and are very interesting in the way that they grow.** *Mustard* **begins with the letter M, and today we'll learn why Jesus**

used mustard seeds as a great example of growing powerful faith!

Hand each child a mustard seed and caution kids to be careful not to lose the tiny seeds. Say: **Mustard seeds are one of the tiniest seeds God created—but they miraculously grow into incredibly large and sturdy trees! The black mustard tree is probably the one spoken of in the Bible, and it grew to be twelve feet tall or taller. Mustard plants were first used for their spicy seeds over two thousand years ago. Cooks in New Testament times used mustard to spice up the meats and vegetables they served. Powdered dry mustard is still a common kitchen spice today, and the yellow mustard we eat on hot dogs today is a mixture of powdered mustard, salt, spices, and lemon or vinegar.**

But the most amazing thing about mustard isn't the taste—it's the size of a mustard seed compared with the huge tree it grows! From one tiny mustard seed, hundreds of pounds of mustard can be made! Think about it: every mustard seed starts out tiny but in time grows into a powerful tree that is used for many things. Our faith is the same way! Ask:

- **How is faith like a mustard seed?**
- **In what ways does faith grow and grow?**

Say: **Let's see what Jesus says about having faith the size of a mustard seed.**

READING THE WORD

Invite a volunteer to read aloud Matthew 17:20 and Luke 17:5, 6. Say: **Wow! Jesus told us that even if our faith begins small like a mustard seed, it is big enough to accomplish great things!** Ask:

- **In what ways does knowing and following Jesus help our faith grow?**
- **How does faith help us conquer problems? love others? obey God?**

Say: **In the same way that a mustard seed grows from something small into a powerful tree, our faith may begin small but can grow into a powerful faith that can accomplish great things for Jesus! Let's plant mini mustard gardens to remind us that our faith is a living, growing thing that blooms when we know and follow Jesus.**

Hand each child a plastic vial, then have kids use fine-tipped permanent markers to write "Faith Grows!" on their vials. For each mini mustard garden, soak two cotton balls in water. Loosely wrap several mustard seeds in the wet cotton, then gently place the cotton and seeds in the vial. Close the top on the vial. Tape the ends of a satin cord to opposite sides of the vial near the top so kids can wear the mustard gardens as necklaces. Remind kids to water their seeds a bit every day or two. When the seeds sprout and become too tall for the vial, remove the lid and plant the tiny plants in potting soil.

End by sharing a prayer thanking Jesus for helping our faith grow into a powerful force to be used for his glory!

NATIVITY
Let's celebrate Jesus every day!
Luke 2:1-20; 1 Peter 1:8, 9

A TO Z SUPPLIES: You'll need a Bible, a crèche scene (or a nativity Christmas ornament), scissors, glue, medium-sized boxes, and a variety of papers with texture, including sandpaper, gift wrap, aluminum foil, wallpaper, construction paper, and brown paper sacks.

Before class, cut the four sides from boxes and be sure there's a box side for each child. Cut the centers from the box sides to make 2-inch-wide frames.

SPELLING IT OUT

Hand out the box frames and invite kids to hold the frames around their faces as if they're on television. Invite kids to briefly tell about when and where they were born. (If your class is very large, form groups of three and have kids tell each other their stories in small groups.)

When the birthday stories are told, say: **Birthdays are wonderful, aren't they? And everyone's birthday is a bit different. Some people are born in hospitals, some in houses, and some may even be born in unusual places**

such as a car. **Think about Jesus' birthday for a moment.** Pause, then ask:

- **Where was Jesus born?**
- **Who was with Jesus when he was born?**

Say: **Jesus' birthday story is what we often call the Christmas story or the nativity.** Point out the crèche or nativity ornament and say: **Around Christmas you'll often see scenes like this. They are called nativity scenes because they show all the different people and animals around Jesus just after he was born.** *Nativity* **begins with the letter N, and today we'll learn more about the nativity and why the nativity changed the world forever!**

READING THE WORD

Invite kids to hold up their frames and retell the Christmas story in their own words. (If you prefer or if kids need help, invite several volunteers to read the story from Luke 2:1-20.)

Say: **The story and events of Christmas and the nativity changed the world forever. Nothing was the same again. Now we have a glorious reason to celebrate all year long, every year of our lives!** Read aloud Hebrews 12:2 and 1 Peter 1:8, 9. Then ask:

- **In what ways did Jesus' birth change the world? help people? bring us love?**
- **How can we celebrate Jesus and his love every day, not just at Christmas?**

Say: **Let's make a nativity scene of our own to remind us of the special night that changed the world. In fact, you can leave this nativity scene up all year long to remind you to celebrate Jesus every day and not just at Christmas!**

Have children use scissors and the different textures of paper to make the following nativity elements: Mary, Joseph, the star, the manger and baby Jesus, and several animals. Glue the elements to the box frame. Tell kids to hang or set their nativity scenes in a place where they'll be seen every day. End with a prayer thanking Jesus for changing the world with his love. Then joyously sing "Happy Birthday" to Jesus.

OUTER GARMENT

Give freely to others.
Proverbs 22:9; Luke 6:29, 30

A TO Z SUPPLIES: You'll need a Bible, a coat, solid-colored shower curtains, scissors, and permanent markers.

Before class, make sure you have a solid-colored shower curtain for every six kids. Kids will be making neat outer garments, so if you'd like large garments, use a shower curtain for every four kids. If you just want an outer garment cape, one shower curtain will work for eight kids. Choose either white or colored shower curtains.

SPELLING IT OUT

Put on your coat and walk around the room as you say: **I'm wearing one of the most important pieces of clothing in New Testament times. It wasn't as heavy as this coat, but it was used in many of the same ways. This clothing was called an outer garment because it was worn outside of clothes.** *Outer* **begins with the letter O, and today we'll learn about the importance of outer garments and why Jesus told us to give away our coats if someone asked.**

The outer garment was often called a cloak and was much like a long jacket made of woven cotton, wool, or flax. Outer garments were dyed in a variety of colors and were very important to wear. In fact, a Jewish man could not enter the temple if he wasn't wearing his outer garment. According to the Old Testament, some outer garments had a blue border and fringe, which was meant to remind people of God's commandments (Numbers 15:37-41). **The outer garment was a prized possession because it protected the wearer from the hot sun, sandstorms, and wind—it could even be slept on when needed. That's why it was against God's law to keep a poor person's outer garment overnight—even if he owed you money. In other words, these garments were treasured and very important to the wearer.** Ask:

- ■ **How would it feel if a stranger asked someone for his outer garment?**
- ■ **Would it be easy to give it away? Explain.**

N
O
P
Q
R
S
T
U
V
W
X
Y
Z

Say: **Let's see what Jesus and the Bible say about freely giving to others.**

READING THE WORD

Ask for several volunteers to read aloud Luke 6:29b, 30; Proverbs 22:9; and 2 Corinthians 9:11. Then say: **Wow! Jesus wants us to freely give even the most important things we have to people who need them! That's pretty powerful—and it might be hard to do!** Ask:

■ **How does freely giving to others demonstrate our love for them? for Jesus?**

■ **Why is it important to give to others and to help when they ask?**

Say: **When Jesus said we should give away a cloak if someone asked for it, he was telling us to be generous and giving even when it is hard. But giving freely to others is what Jesus wants us to do. After all, Jesus freely gave his life for us! We can make cool outer garments to wear and remind us of giving to others willingly and lovingly.**

To make cloaks, let kids cut 2-foot-wide strips down the length of the shower curtain, from top to bottom. Invite kids to use permanent markers to decorate the outer garments. Encourage kids to write a sentence of their own that sums us what Jesus told us about giving to others. For example, sentences might read, "Give freely to others" or "Jesus wants us to share willingly." Wear your outer garments as you offer a prayer to the Lord asking for his help in always being ready and willing to give to others.

 # POTTER
God shapes and molds us.
Isaiah 64:8; Romans 9:20, 21

A TO Z SUPPLIES: You'll need a Bible, premoistened towelettes, aluminum foil, modeling clay, and edible modeling dough (see recipe below).

Before class, make several batches of edible modeling dough using the following recipe: For every ten kids, mix ²/₃ cup of sweetened condensed milk, 4½ cups powdered sugar, and sev-

eral drops of food coloring (your choice). Knead the ingredients until they're smooth and pliable. Store the edible dough in airtight bags or plastic containers with lids.

SPELLING IT OUT

Take a portion of modeling clay and form the following objects, inviting kids to guess the shapes you're molding:

- a bowl or cup
- a flower
- a bird
- a heart

Say: **Clay is fun to make things from. People who earn a living making clay pots, vases, and figurines are called potters.** *Potter* **begins with the letter P, and today we'll discover why potters were important in New Testament times. We'll also learn that God is our Potter who can mold and form us according to his will.**

As you talk, form a jug from the clay that you're holding. Say: **Pottery in New Testament times included vases, cups, bottles, jugs, and jars. Clay was formed and molded into the desired shape, then smoothed and made beautiful by rubbing pieces of stone or seashell over the clay as it turned on a potter's wheel. After being baked in hot ovens or even dried in the sunshine, the clay became hard and could be used to hold various grains or liquids.** Hold up the clay jug you've formed. **Let's see what the Bible says about God being our Potter and how we're like clay in his hands.**

READING THE WORD

Invite volunteers to read aloud Psalm 119:73; Isaiah 64:8; and Romans 9:20, 21. Then ask:

- **In what ways are we like clay in God's hands?**
- **Why is it good that God is the one molding us?**
- **How does God form us to use in his service?**

Say: **God is our Potter, and we are the clay in his hands. God forms us and smoothes us into people he can use to accomplish his plans. Through hard times and through good times, God is shaping us to be the kind of people he can use for his will.** Ask:

- **What kind of people does God desire us to be?**
- **How does God help us become that kind of person? How does Jesus help us?**

31

Hand kids premoistened towelettes to clean their hands. Put down pieces of aluminum foil for kids to work on, then distribute walnut-sized balls of edible modeling dough. Say: **Let's mold and form tasty hearts to remind us how we are molded and shaped by God and his love to accomplish his plans.**

Allow kids several minutes to form their hearts. Before nibbling your tasty treats, share a prayer thanking God for being the Potter and asking for his help in being molded into the kind of people God can use to accomplish his will.

 # QUIET
Being still helps us listen to God.
Psalm 46:10; Matthew 6:6; Luke 5:16

A TO Z SUPPLIES: You'll need a Bible, a large seashell, permanent markers, glitter-glue pens, and a seashell for each child.

Before class, collect a seashell for each child, preferably the curled or hollow type you can listen to. If you can't locate seashells, use small, clear plastic drinking cups that kids can decorate as pretend seashells.

SPELLING IT OUT

Have kids sit in a circle, then pass the seashell around the circle, inviting each child to listen to the shell for a moment. Ask the children to be very still and silent as you pass the shell. When everyone has had a turn to listen to the seashell, ask:

■ **What did you hear as you listened to the shell?**
■ **Can we really hear the ocean in a seashell? Explain.**

Say: **What we really hear are quiet sounds that we normally can't hear until we block out louder sounds, like with a seashell. It almost sounds likes the ocean, doesn't it? It's amazing what we can hear when we take the time to be still and quiet. The word *quiet* begins with the letter Q, and today we'll explore how being quiet and still helps us listen to God. We'll also learn that Jesus took time to be alone and still with God.**

Pass the seashell around the circle as you speak. **Wherever Jesus went, large crowds followed him.** Instruct kids to stop passing the shell, then ask the child holding it, "Why did crowds follow Jesus?" Continue: **Jesus was so busy teaching and help-ing others that it wasn't always easy to be quiet and still. But Jesus knew that it's important to spend quiet time with God.** Stop passing the shell and ask the child holding it, "How does quiet time with God help us?" Continue: **Jesus spent his quiet time with God in prayer and in being still so he could listen to God speak to his heart. Jesus knew that being quiet and still helps us hear God in our lives.** Stop passing the shell and ask the child holding it, "How does being quiet and still help us hear God?" Then say: **Let's see what the Bible says about being quiet and still before God.**

READING THE WORD

Read aloud Psalm 46:10; Matthew 6:6; and Luke 5:16. Then say: **When we're quiet and still before God, we realize how awesome and powerful he is. And we can begin to listen to God. When we're surrounded by busyness and noise, we can't listen to anything—especially God!** Ask:

- **How can we be quiet and still before God?**
- **Why is it important to have quiet time with God?**
- **In what ways does taking time to be still before God show him our love?**

Let kids decorate seashells with glitter-glue pens or perma-nent markers (or make pretend seashells from small, clear plas-tic cups). Encourage kids to write or draw things that will help them remember to spend quiet time with God. As kids deco-rate their shells, have them remain silent and relatively still. Then ask kids to share what thoughts about God might have gone through their minds and hearts as they worked.

After everyone has had a chance to share, challenge kids to listen to the quiet of the seashells each day before they take five minutes to be still and silent before God.

ROCK
Jesus is our rock and foundation!
Matthew 7:24-27; 1 Corinthians 3:11

A TO Z SUPPLIES: You'll need a Bible, a large rock, a medium-sized box, a balloon, smooth stones (about 4-inches long), glitter glue, crayons, craft glue, and squares of craft felt.

Before class, collect a rock large enough for a child to stand on and one small, smooth stone for each child. Blow up and tie off the balloon.

SPELLING IT OUT

Place the balloon, the box, and the large rock on the floor in the center of the room. Invite kids to sit in a circle around the items. Ask for three volunteers to help you with the object talk, then instruct each volunteer to stand beside one of the items.

Say: **We're going to have a little contest here. In a moment, we're going to see which item makes the best foundation to stand on: a balloon, an empty box, or a rock. But first, let's vote on the foundation you think will be strongest.** Have learners give thumbs up or down as you point to each item. Then have the volunteers try to stand on their items. Of course, the box will squish and the balloon will pop!

While the child stands on the rock, say: **Wow! This rock really makes a sturdy foundation!** *Rock* **begins with the letter R, and today we'll discover more about what rocks were used for in New Testament times and how Jesus is more solid than even a rock for building our lives on.**

Rocks and stones were used in many ways in the New Testament. The most common rocks used in building things were made of marble, limestone, basalt, flint, and granite. Piled close together, rocks made sturdy, protective walls. Laid side by side and in a large square shape, rocks provided houses and shelters for livestock. And rocky soil made a good, sturdy place to build even wooden houses. Since rock was hard and lasted for years, people in New Testament times knew the best place to build their houses was on a rock-solid foundation. Read aloud Matthew 7:24-27, then ask:

■ **Why is rock a good place to build on?**
■ **In what ways is Jesus like a sturdy rock?**

Say: **The Bible gives many references to God and Jesus being our rock-solid foundations and fortresses. Let's see what the Bible says about Jesus being our foundation.**

READING THE WORD

Invite volunteers to read aloud 1 Corinthians 3:11 and 2 Timothy 2:19. Then ask:

- What does is mean to build our lives on Jesus?
- Why are we wise to build our lives on Jesus?
- How does knowing that Jesus is our rock-solid foundation help strengthen our faith?

Say: **If we build our lives on flimsy things such as money or being famous, we'll collapse because our flimsy foundation will collapse. But with Jesus as our foundation, we'll stand firm forever! Let's make firm foundation paperweights to remind us of how we're to build our lives on Jesus.**

Hand each child a small, smooth stone. Invite kids to use glitter glue and crayons to decorate their smooth stones. Have kids use glitter to write "1 Cor. 3:11" on their stones, then glue a small square of craft felt to the bottoms of the stones to prevent scratches on desks or tables.

Challenge kids to use the firm foundation paperweights at home or school as a reminder that Jesus is the only solid foundation on which to build their lives. End with a prayer thanking God for providing Jesus, our rock-solid foundation for life here and in heaven.

SAMARITAN
We can love all people.
Matthew 5:44; John 4:7-14, 27

A TO Z SUPPLIES: You'll need a Bible, pictures of people cut from magazines, new craft sticks, small sandwich bags, tape, canned icing, small ready-made cookies, and plastic knives.

Before class, be sure you have enough supplies for every child to have at least four cookies and two craft sticks.

SPELLING IT OUT

Line the magazine pictures up on the floor or tape them to a wall for kids to see. Gather kids around the pictures, then challenge them to compare and contrast the people in the pictures by answering questions such as "What makes us all alike?" "How are we different?" and "How are we all special in God's eyes?"

After a minute or two of discussion, say: **There are lots of people in the world, aren't there? We're from different**

N
O
P
Q
R
S
T
U
V
W
X
Y
Z

countries. We speak different languages. We even dress differently. But no one is better than anyone else because God has made us all! Unfortunately, not everyone believes this. In New Testament times, there was a small country or region called Samaria. *Samaria* begins with the letter S, and today we'll discover why the Israelites didn't like the Samaritans. We'll also learn why Jesus wants us to love and accept all people.

Samaria had many different people living it from many different races and who worshiped many different gods. Because of this, the Israelites, or Jews, didn't like the Samaritans and would never help them. Ask:

- Do you think it was right to treat the Samaritans badly simply because they were different? Why or why not?
- How do you think Jesus would have treated a Samaritan?

Continue: **Jesus recognized that we are all different, but he also knew that God wants us all to love one another. Listen to what happened when Jesus met a woman from Samaria at a well.**

READING THE WORD

Read aloud John 4:7-14, 27 or retell the account of Jesus and the woman at the well in your own words. Then ask:

- Why did Jesus accept the woman even though she was from Samaria?
- What did Jesus' disciples learn about treating all people with kindness and respect? What can we learn?

Say: **The people with Jesus were surprised that he accepted and forgave the woman at the well. They thought Jesus should ignore the woman because she was from Samaria. But Jesus demonstrated his love for all people—even for the most unlovable—and Jesus wants us to be kind to all people, too.** Read aloud Matthew 5:44 and Ephesians 4:32, then ask:

- Why is it good to be loving and kind to others?
- How is loving others a way to show our love for Jesus?

Say: **It's not always easy to love others, especially when they're unkind to us, but that's exactly what Jesus commands us to do. And oh, how sweet it feels when we** spread Jesus' love to others! Let's make sweet people pops to share with someone and remind us that it's sweet to treat others with love and respect.

Have kids spread icing between two cookies and insert a new craft stick to make a cookie lollipop. Slide the cookie pop into a clear sandwich bag and pull the bag tight over the cookie. Tape the bag around the craft-stick "neck." Finally, tape one of the magazine faces to the plastic bag. Have kids make one to eat and one to give to someone during the week.

End by holding your people pops up and offering a prayer asking God's help in showing you ways to be sweet and kind to all people.

TEACHER

Jesus is our best teacher.
Mark 4:1, 2; Luke 2:46, 47; John 14:23

A TO Z SUPPLIES: You'll need a Bible, a chalkboard, white chalk, black and brown construction paper, glue, scissors, and hair spray.

Before class, be sure you have one piece of chalk for every two kids.

SPELLING IT OUT

Gather kids by the chalkboard and draw five spaces on the chalkboard side by side. (You'll be spelling out the name "Jesus" on the spaces.) Tell kids you have a letter game to play to find the name of our most important teacher. Invite kids to guess letters of the alphabet and fill in the blanks as the correct letters are named.

When the name "Jesus" has been spelled, say: **Jesus wasn't just our Savior and friend, he was also our best teacher. The word *teacher* begins with the letter T, and today we'll learn what kinds of things Jesus taught us and how we learn from our best teacher every day. When you hear one of the things Jesus taught about, raise your hand.**

N O P Q R S T U V W X Y Z

Continue: **Jesus was often called "rabbi" by his friends and followers.** *Rabbi* **was a Hebrew word that meant "master" or "learned man," so many people used it when they wanted to address a teacher. Jesus was a master at how God wants us to live and obey, which is why people called him "rabbi." Jesus taught us about loving and obeying God.** (Pause for kids to raise their hands, then choose two volunteers to write the words "love" and "obey" on the chalkboard.) **Jesus also taught us about being kind to one another and serving each other and God.** (Have two more children write "kindness" and "serving" on the board.) **In Luke 11, Jesus taught his disciples and us how to pray.** (Have a volunteer write "pray" on the board.) **Finally, Jesus also taught us how to be forgiving.** (Write the word "forgiving" on the board.) **Wow! Just look at what our best teacher taught us!** Ask:

■ **Why was Jesus such a perfect teacher?**
■ **How does Jesus' teaching help us live?**

Say: **Let's see what else the Bible says about Jesus as our best teacher and what we can learn from following him.**

READING THE WORD

Read aloud Mark 4:1, 2; Luke 2:46, 47; and John 14:23. Say: **Jesus taught us by his words as well as his actions. So when we see how Jesus forgave others, we can learn how to forgive. When we see examples of how Jesus obeyed God, we learn about obeying, too.** Ask:

■ **Why is obeying Jesus' teaching important?**
■ **How can we keep learning from Jesus?**

Say: **Reading the Bible and praying help us keep learning what Jesus taught. Let's make cool chalkboard posters to remind us how Jesus is the best teacher we'll ever have.**

Hand each child a half sheet of black construction paper and a half sheet of brown construction paper. Have kids cut about 1 inch from each side of their black papers, then glue the black papers to the brown papers to make paper "slates." Instruct kids to use white chalk to write "Jesus is our best teacher!" on the black construction paper. Finally, spray the papers with hair spray to keep the chalk from smearing.

When kids finish the chalkboards, end with a prayer thanking Jesus for teaching us with his perfect love. Encourage kids to hang the posters in their rooms or school lockers to remind them to continue to learn from the best teacher ever, Jesus.

UPPER ROOM

We want to remember Jesus.
Luke 22:7-13, 19, 20

A TO Z SUPPLIES: You'll need a Bible, disposable plastic goblets and plates (one of each for every child), colored electrical tape, scissors, fine-tipped permanent markers, a small loaf of bread, and a pitcher of water.

Before class, plan to have your children's minister or a church leader visit your class to talk about how the Lord's Supper is celebrated in your church. In this object talk, you'll be nibbling bread and water as a symbolic Lord's Supper.

SPELLING IT OUT

Place a plastic goblet and plate on a table or on the floor and gather kids around. Ask kids to tell what these items are used for, then say: **It looks as if we're getting ready for a special meal. In a moment, you can help set the table as we learn about a special supper Jesus and his disciples shared in a place called the upper room.** *Upper* **begins with the letter U, and today we'll discover what was important about the upper room. We'll also learn that Jesus wants us to always remember him in a very special way.**

When Jesus arrived in Jerusalem for the last time, he knew that he was soon going to die on the cross for us. So Jesus wanted to share one last supper with his friends. It was time for a very special Jewish feast, Passover, so Jesus instructed his disciples to prepare for the feast.

Read aloud Luke 22:7-13. Then have kids help you set the table or prepare your "table" on the floor by setting out the plastic goblets and plates. Ask kids to be seated and continue: **Jesus wanted us to remember him in a very special way and to remember all he has done for us. Let's read a bit about what happened in the upper room and how this special supper for Jesus and his disciples turned into one of our most beloved Christian celebrations.**

READING THE WORD

Ask for a volunteer to read aloud Luke 22:19, 20. Then invite the children's minister or church leader to explain about the

celebration of the Lord's Supper in your church. Serve the bread and water as the celebration is being explained.

When the leader is finished, ask:

■ **How is the Lord's Supper a good way to remember Jesus and all he has done for us?**

■ **What other ways can we remember Jesus and his love?**

Say: **Jesus died for us so our sins can be forgiven and so we can live forever with God in heaven. Jesus taught us how to love God and one another. And Jesus helps us every day through our troubles and sadness. In other words, Jesus is our best friend—and someone we never want to forget or take for granted! Let's make neat goblets and plates to use when we eat and remind us of the special supper Jesus shared in the upper room.**

Have kids use permanent markers to write "Remember me" on their plates and "Luke 22:19, 20" on their goblets. Then use colored electrical tape to decorate the plates and goblets with colorful designs and confetti.

End by giving thanks for Jesus and for the wonderful gift of the Lord's Supper.

 # VICTORY
We have the victory with Jesus!
1 Corinthians 15:57; 1 Timothy 6:12

A TO Z SUPPLIES: You'll need a Bible, palm branch (available from most florists), paper cups, plastic spoons, ice cubes, cleaned celery stalks, maraschino cherries, orange juice, raspberry gelatin mix, and pineapple juice.

Before class, check with a florist or flower department for palm branches. A potted palm-tree branch will work just fine. Kids will be making Victory Punch in this object talk.

SPELLING IT OUT

Have kids sit in a circle, then hold up the palm frond. Ask kids to identify the type of branch you're holding. Say: **This is a palm branch or frond, and it was a symbol of victory in New Testament times. *Victory* begins with the letter V, and today we'll discover when people in Jesus' time waved or used palm branches. We'll also learn that we**

have victory over sin and death when we know, love, and follow Jesus.

Pass the palm branch around the circle and tell kids that, each time they hear the word *victory,* the person holding the palm is to wave it. Say: **Palm trees grow all over the biblical lands and provide shade as well as dates and figs for the people. Some palm trees live to be over two hundred years old, and their branches, or fronds, will grow over ten feet long! People in Jesus' day knew that palm trees continued to grow and produce fruit in dry, hot weather. In other words, palm trees had *victory* over the weather. Because of this, palm branches soon came to symbolize *victory.* People would wave them after battles to show *victory* over enemies. And when Jesus rode into Jerusalem the last time, the people lined the road and waved palm branches. Why did they do this? What *victory* were they celebrating?**

Allow kids time to respond, then continue passing the palm branch: **Jesus had come to Jerusalem to die for our sins, and although the people didn't know then, they were giving the sign for *victory* as respect to Jesus and to show that they knew he had come in the name of the Lord.**

READING THE WORD

Read aloud 1 Corinthians 15:57 and 1 Timothy 6:12. Say: **These are powerful and important verses because they tell us that we have victory over sin and death when we accept Jesus into our lives. When we accept and follow Jesus, we defeat the power of sin and will have eternal life. Now that's victory!** Ask:

- **What other victories do we have when we follow Jesus?**
- **How does it feel to know that we've won the fight over evil when we accept and love Jesus?**
- **How can we help other people join in the victory?**

Say: **What a great feeling we have to know that we have victory with Jesus! It makes me feel like celebrating. So let's make delicious Victory Punch to celebrate our victory in Jesus.**

Hand each child a paper cup and follow the simple recipe below to make victory punch. (Either read the recipe aloud or, if you prefer, write the recipe on newsprint for kids to follow.) Have kids mix the punch right in their cups.

Vessels (drinking glass or cup)
Ice cubes (2)
Celery stalk "palm branch"
Two cherries
Orange juice (fill half the cup)
Raspberry gelatin mix (1 spoonful)
Yellow pineapple juice (fill rest of the cup)

Before enjoying your punch together, share a prayer thanking Jesus for the miraculous victory we have through his love, forgiveness, and salvation!

WIDOW
Give to God from your heart.
Mark 12:41-44; 2 Corinthians 9:7

A TO Z SUPPLIES: You'll need a Bible, pennies, scissors, aluminum-foil pie pans, colored electrical tape, and staplers.

Before class, be sure you have two pennies and two aluminum-foil pie pans for each child.

SPELLING IT OUT

Hand each child two pennies and say: **Pretend that this is all the money you had in the world. Pretend that you've kept good care of your two coins and know you may never have any more coins than the two you're holding.** (Pause.) **In a moment, we'll learn how important two small coins were to a widow. A widow is a woman whose husband has died.** *Widow* **begins with the letter W, and today we'll learn about how widows were treated in New Testament times. We'll also discover that the best way to give to God is through our joy and love.**

Back in Jesus' day, widows were often poor because the husbands who had provided for them were no longer alive. It was often hard for widows to find enough food to eat—let alone a place to stay or new clothes to wear. The early church knew that widows needed special help, so they set up groups of people to see that widows' needs were met.

Jesus also knew how much help widows needed and how little money they had. One day Jesus was watching

people put money in the collection plate at the temple. Rich people gave a lot, but when a poor widow came to give, she gave two coins a bit like the pennies you're holding, only worth less. Jesus told his disciples that the woman had given more than the rich people because the rich people only gave God a portion of what they had. The poor widow gave all she had to God. Ask:

- Why do you think the widow gave all she had to God?
- How was the poor widow's gift a gift of love to God?

Say: Let's see what the Bible says about giving to God.

READING THE WORD

Invite a volunteer to read aloud 2 Corinthians 9:7 and 1 Timothy 6:18. Then ask:

- Why is it important to give cheerfully and generously?
- In what ways does our attitude affect our giving?

Say: God wants us to be generous, cheerful givers just as the poor widow was. The widow didn't have much to give, but she willingly gave all she had to God. God knows what is in our hearts, and when he sees a generous spirit and happy sharing, it makes God smile, too! Let's make special offering-plate banks to hold the coins that we cheerfully want to give to God and others.

Help children carefully snip an opening in the center of one pie pan large enough for coins to go through. Then staple two pie pans together to make a hollow bank. Let kids use bits of colored tape to decorate their offering-plate banks. Have kids place their pennies inside the banks and challenge kids to give to God from the money they earn from allowances, babysitting, or other odd jobs.

 ## X RAY
The Lord knows our hearts!
Jeremiah 12:3; Matthew 23:26

A TO Z SUPPLIES: You'll need a Bible, a dirty cup, an X ray (available free from clinics or hospitals), scissors, tape, fishing line, markers, and red construction paper.

A
B
C
D
E
F
G
H
I
J
K
L
M

Before class, prepare a coffee cup with leftover coffee or food stains inside. The cup should appear clean on the outside. You'll need one large X ray or several small ones, since you'll be cutting the X rays into heart shapes for each child.

SPELLING IT OUT

Gather kids and hold up the X ray. Ask kids what you're holding and what X rays allow us to see. Then say: **X rays are pretty neat, aren't they? They let us see on the inside what our eyes can't see from the outside. X rays can help us know if there's a problem or illness or hurt inside us and maybe how to help the hurt.** *X ray* **begins with the letter X, and today we'll discover how Jesus is like a powerful X-ray machine for our hearts. But first, let's look at a cup I brought and see what you can see.**

Hold the cup so kids can see the outside, but not the inside. Ask them to describe the cup and what they might like to sip from it, such as milk, juice, or soft drinks. Then ask the kids how an X ray might help us know if the cup is really okay to sip from.

Show kids the inside of the cup and say: **Wow! This cup looked clean on the outside, but it's not clean inside, is it? X-ray vision could have helped us see what was on the inside, but we don't have X-ray vision. However, Jesus does! Jesus can see what we're like on the inside—even if we need healing from hurt feelings, sadness, or anger we may be carrying inside and may not even know is there. We might be one way on the outside but feel very differently on the inside. Let's see what the Bible tells us about how the Lord knows us inside and out!**

READING THE WORD

Ask kids to read aloud Jeremiah 12:3a; Psalm 24:3, 4a; and Matthew 23:26b. Then say: **We may have hurt feelings and sadness inside and not even know it. But Jesus knows because he can see what is in our hearts and he knows what we are thinking and feeling, too.** Ask:

■ **How does it feel to know Jesus sees inside us?**

■ **In what ways can Jesus help us when he knows what's in our hearts and minds?**

■ **How does knowing that Jesus knows our hearts draw us closer to him? strengthen our faith?**

Hold up the X ray once more and say: **Jesus is almost like a powerful X-ray machine of love. Jesus sees where we hurt, and he knows how to help us. That makes me feel good and very loved indeed! Let's make our own X-ray hearts to remind us of how Jesus sees inside our hearts and feelings.**

Help kids cut heart shapes from the X ray. (Each child should have one heart at least 4 inches wide.) Then have each child cut out one paper heart from the red construction and write on the heart, "Jesus sees inside my heart!" Tape a 5-inch length of fishing line to the red heart and tape the other end to the X-ray heart. Then tape a 10-inch length of fishing line to the top of the X-ray heart to use as a hanger. Challenge kids to hang the heart from a light fixture, a window, or a doorway to remind them that Jesus knows them from the inside out!

YOKE
Jesus fits his love to each of us.
Matthew 11:29, 30; John 13:34

A TO Z SUPPLIES: You'll need a Bible, a picture of oxen in a yoke, twist-tie wires, and small seed beads.

Before class, choose twist-tie wires that you can peel the paper from to reveal just the wire. Purchase seed beads in a variety of colors.

SPELLING IT OUT

Gather kids and draw a sideways "B" on the chalkboard or on a sheet of newsprint. Ask kids if they know what you've drawn, then give the following clues.

I'm made for oxen and fit just right—
Not too loose and not too tight.

After kids share their guesses, say: **I've drawn a "yoke." It's used to help two oxen stay close together as they plow fields or pull wagons.** *Yoke* **begins with the letter Y, and today we'll learn more about yokes the people in New Testament times used and made. We'll also discover that Jesus custom-fits his love for each one of us.**

Show kids the picture of the yoke of oxen and see if they can locate the yoke in the picture. Say: **Yokes were made of wood, but the truly amazing thing is that the openings for the oxen's heads were hand carved to fit each ox perfectly. The openings in the yoke fit over the oxen's heads and fit them just right as they kept the oxen side by side. Let's see how yokes worked.** Have pairs of kids stand side by side and link their elbows. Then challenge kids to walk to one end of the room and back, staying side by side the entire way.

When kids return to their places, say: **It made plowing and pulling much easier to have the oxen stay close together. But the important part was having a yoke that fit just right! Oxen are very strong—they can pull nearly two to three times their weight. If a yoke was too loose or too tight, it would hurt the oxen as they plowed the fields or pulled heavy carts. So yokes had to be made with great care, patience, and thought for the animals. You know, Jesus probably learned woodworking from Joseph, who was a carpenter. Some Bible students believe that Jesus may even have made wooden yokes. One thing is for sure—Jesus knew about custom-fits! Let's see what Jesus said about his yoke.**

READING THE WORD

Invite several volunteers to read aloud Matthew 11:29, 30 and John 13:34. Then ask:

■ **What do you suppose Jesus meant by his "yoke"?**

■ **How does Jesus guide us as a yoke guides oxen?**

Say: **Jesus knows what's best for each of us, so he makes his love, healing, and even his help fit each of us differently. Jesus healed people in many different ways, and he taught us in many ways, too. That's because Jesus knows we're all different and respond to things differently. Just as a yoke was custom-fit to guide, help, and not hurt oxen, Jesus' love is custom-fit to guide, help, and not hurt us! Isn't it wonderful that Jesus custom-fits his love to every one of us in ways we can feel and understand? Let's make custom-fit rings to wear around our fingers as a reminder of the way Jesus custom-fits his love around our lives.**

Set out the small seed beads and hand each child a twist-tie wire to make a custom-fit ring. Invite children to string several seed beads on the twist-tie wires. Challenge kids to use colors that will symbolize Jesus' love, such as red for love, green for everlasting life, and white for Jesus' forgiveness. When the beads are strung, have kids custom-fit the rings to fit their fingers, then twist the ends of the wires together to hold the beads on the ring.

ZACCHAEUS

We can forgive others as Jesus did.
Luke 19:1-10; Ephesians 4:32

A TO Z SUPPLIES: You'll need a Bible, photocopies of Zacchaeus (on page 48), markers, tape, newspapers, and green construction paper.

Before class, slightly enlarge and photocopy the illustration of Zacchaeus for each child plus one extra. Color one of the characters and cut it out. Tape the figure of Zacchaeus in the classroom in plain sight and up high, such as near the ceiling, on a light fixture, or at the top of a door. You'll also need to collect about eight sheets of newspaper for each child.

SPELLING IT OUT

Gather kids and say: **We have a pretend visitor in our class today, but he is a bit hard to see. Our visitor's name is Zacchaeus, and he's very small. In fact, you'll have to look hard to find him. When you spot Zacchaeus, jump up and say, "I spy Zacchaeus!"**

When everyone has located Zacchaeus, retrieve the paper figure and tape him to the wall beside you. Say: ***Zacchaeus* begins with the letter Z, and today we will learn how a small man named Zacchaeus learned to have a big heart through Jesus' forgiveness. We'll also learn that we can forgive others just as Jesus did.**

Retell the story of Zacchaeus from Luke 19:1-10, having kids squat low each time you say the name *Zacchaeus.*

When you're finished retelling the story of how Jesus forgave Zacchaeus, say: **When Jesus forgave Zacchaeus for taking people's money and being unkind, Zacchaeus's heart grew! Because of Jesus' love and forgiveness, Zacchaeus felt good and new and wanted to make things right.** Ask:

ABCDEFGHIJKLM

■ How did Jesus' forgiveness demonstrate his love?
■ In what ways can forgiving others draw us closer to
  Jesus? to others?

Say: **Offering someone forgiveness shows that we have
a lot of love. It also shows respect for others, kindness,
and obedience to Jesus. Let's see what God's Word says
about forgiveness.**

READING THE WORD

Invite volunteers to read aloud Ephesians 4:32 and
Colossians 3:13. Then ask:

■ Why should we forgive others over and over?
■ How can forgiveness lead to peace? to love? to more
  forgiveness?

Say: **When we offer someone forgiveness, it makes
them feel good. And it sets a loving example, just as Jesus
did when he forgave others. Once someone is forgiven,
the chances are good that person will be more forgiving
of others, too. That's pretty neat, isn't it? Forgiveness just
grows and grows! Forgiving others isn't always easy, but
forgiveness is exactly what Jesus wants us to give to others. Let's make forgiveness trees that remind us not only
how Jesus forgave Zacchaeus that day but also how good
forgiveness feels when we give it to others today.**

For each tree, lay six to eight newspapers end to end and overlapped at the ends
about 2-inches. Roll the papers from one
end to the other and tape the side of the
roll. (Tape the entire seam.) Make six 6-inch
cuts at the top of the roll, then gently pull
the layers at the cut end. The tree will
slowly "grow" and extend as you pull.
Continue pulling until the tree is about 2½-
feet tall. Tear green construction paper into
leaves and have kids write on each leaf
something positive that comes from forgiveness, such as love, kindness, healing, help,
encouragement, and more forgiveness.
Finally, tape the leaves to the ends of the
newspaper "branches" and tape the picture
of Zacchaeus somewhere in the tree.